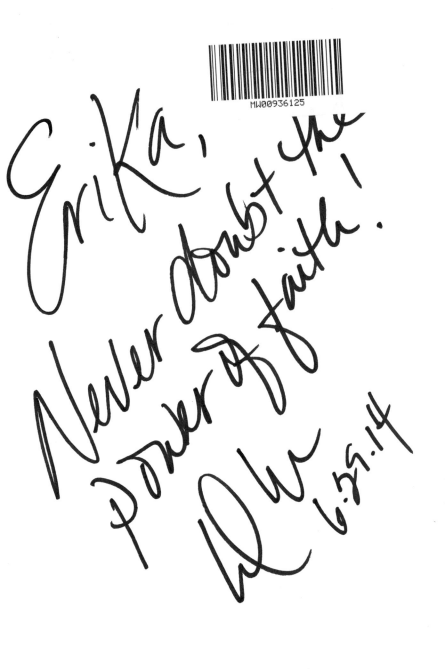

Erika,

Never doubt the
power of faith.

6.29.14

MW00936125

INMATE 1142980

"The Desiree Lee Story"

Presentation Topics by the Author:

IMAGINE|CREATE|BECOME

Eliminate Fear to Become Fearless

Annual 10 City Prison Prevention Tour

*Season of Preparation: Seize Opportunity &
Step into Your Greatness*

INMATE 1142980

"The Desiree Lee Story"

INMATE 1142980 "The Desiree Lee Story"

Copyright ©2014 by I Am Desiree Lee, LLC

Desiree Lee

I Am Desiree Lee, LLC.

Atlanta, GA 30305

www.iamdesireelee.com

Ordering Information

Quantity sales: Special discounts are available on quantity purchases by corporations, associations, and others. For details, contact the publisher at the address above.

Orders by U.S. trade bookstores and wholesalers.

Please contact I Am Desiree Lee, LLC Tel: (404) 919-0396

 www.iamdesireelee.com

Social Media: @dleeinspires

Printed in the United States of America

ISBN-13: 978-1496171528

ISBN-10: 1496171527

I dedicate this book to my lovely daughter. There is a place inside yourself where nothing is impossible!

I also dedicate this book to my loving parents, thank you for believing in my dream to inspire the world. To my brother thank you for pushing me into my purpose!

I love you all more than ever!

TABLE OF CONTENTS

"The Desiree Lee Story"

I was a rebellious child. The one who everyone
was so eager to talk about. The child that always
lashed out. Doing what I wanted to do,
following the one I thought loved me but really
I was playing his fool. This is what began my
story.

Robbing people who had children to feed. It was
their bill money that we were spending on weed.
The devil had me believing that taking what you
want was the right way of living. This is how I
ended up in prison. Listen I have a story to
tell…

Facing the Judge with my life in the palm of her
hands. Regret that I had taken that penitentiary
chance. The sentence 10 years in the state pen.
No way out, only one way in. Listen up young
people! I have a story to tell…

My first time in prison, scared, anxious to get
out of this place. Never did I see my future to

end like this. Marching in a straight line. Left, right, left. Shouting, "Everywhere I go, there is a CO (Correctional Officer) watching me!" I have a story to tell...

Trying to make friends. There I go again trying so hard to be accepted but not comfortable in my own skin. Lights out, my eyes remain open. Aware of those who want to take me as their token. I... have a story to tell...

Fights, rapes, schemes, liars is what I am amongst daily. Screams of help is what I continuously hear in the night. Praying that I won't be their next victim. I have a story that needs to be told...

The sight of correctional officers betting each other for the price of an inmate's sacred place. How they brutally take advantage of our personal privacy and abuse you sexually, unwilling. Force to secrecy, or tossed in the hole. Listen to this truth that is told. I have a story to tell...

On my knees, pleading with God above. I regret how I misused my freedom, so selfish, never took under consideration the lives of love ones. Thought I had it all and now I have nothing. How I stole from stores, and disrespected authority. Please Lord give me another chance. Listen to the sound of my tears my dear friend... I have a story to tell...

When you face that dead end, don't say that you have never been warned. I am pleading with you, while you still have a chance to get it right with the ones who love you. Friends, what about your friends? They are not going to be there in the end. The cells are dark, cold and lonely. Listen to my story before it's yours that will be told.

~Desiree Lee 2005

Y.O.L.O.

You only live once is no longer an
excuse to make careless decisions

Desiree Lee

CHAPTER ONE

In The Pursuit of...

There is a common belief, a universal belief that it is impossible to exceed beyond the mistakes we've once made in our past. We tend to believe this simply because we've seen others who have made similar past decisions in an attempt to surpass these brick walls and failed. Unconsciously, we have adapted to the unwarranted belief system that the average person is not capable of breaking their own personal barriers, incapable of overcoming the wall, of not going any further than what surrounds them at this present moment.

When something happens to the average person, getting fired, not graduating, kicked out the house, told that they will become nothing, or even losing it all, automatically we create reasons to explain or justify to ourselves why this disastrous situation even exists. By saying things like, "That is the way it is," or "That's the way it has always been," and the average person can't see the possibility of it being any different.

I know of this common situation all too well. How do I know you may ask? After trying on many different occasions to fill the emptiness in my life, I began to feel as though I had no more options, and all I had remaining was a criminal background. I found myself retreating into a cold dark place, alone, depressed, and scared. With a huge cloud hanging over my head, reminding me of how I ended up on the wrong side of the law, by making one costly decision.

Before I got off track towards a successful future, my parents were unconditionally giving me valuable advice along my journey. They would say over and over again, "If you lay down with dogs, you'll get up with fleas." "Association brings on assimilation." "Show me who your friends are and I'll show you who you will be." "It's a sin to be pretty and dumb." "If you don't listen to me, you will have to listen to somebody." They were always in my ear about making good decisions, even when I was excelling in school they would say their sayings, which seemed like every single day. I believed that I had life all figured out, but I was wrong, and I didn't listen.

The pursuit of filling these empty voids during my teenage years, almost cost me big time. I found myself in a cell facing 135 years in prison at the age of 17 years old. If only it was possible to go back to that moment, right before I got into my car, and push play in my head so that I could hear the voice of my parents. If only I would have taken ten minutes to think in the most critical moment of my life, going to prison could have been prevented. A ten minute decision that affected my parents, my brother and ultimately my promising future.

It's scary to even think that I could have been released from prison at the age of 152 years old, because of the wrong decision I made at 17 years old. The probability of me living to be 152 years old is slim to none, I would have died in prison. If I would have continued to allow my past mistakes to imprison my mind, all of my dreams and aspirations would have died also.

I knew, as a convicted felon of the hardships that would begin upon my release from prison. Mountains of problems from every side began to arise, until I met the lady with the mustard seed. This single mustard seed reminded me to simply believe. To many, believing is a very difficult thing to do when everything around you is so dark. It was when I believed just one more time, that I saw the brightest light in the darkest place in my life.

My name is Inmate 1142980

I am a convicted felon.

The time that I spent with both of my parents in one household, was in the sunny state of California; these are some of the best memories that I have today. My father, mother, brother and I did everything as a family, we went to church together every Sunday, picnics in the backyard, visits at the park to feed the ducks, and going to the library after school. It was during this time in my life that I felt whole.

My father was a manager at the local grocery store and my mother often traveled out of the state to work. We spent quality time with our father when my mother went to work out of town. My brother and I missed my mother's cooking because my father only knew how to cook a few meals, peanut butter and jelly sandwiches for lunch and spaghetti for dinner. The same meals didn't bother my brother and me so much, just as long as we were with our father.

Some of my best memories with my father were after church on Sunday. He would take us to the 7/11 corner store to get a slushy drink. Cherry flavor was my favorite. In the back seat of the car my brother and I would race to see who would get a brain freeze first. He would always win because I never wanted to drink my whole slushy down in one gulp. This was a special occasion, which was one of many.

When our mother came back in town from work, it was always like she had never left. We would resume our family activities like normal. If our parents argued we never saw it, nor did we ever see them get angry at one another. Our family was picture perfect, like a scene from The Cosby Show, and then something suddenly happened.

On this day, I remember my mother checking me out early from elementary school. On our way to the front office, I turned around and said good-bye to my friends on the playground. I didn't know that my good-bye would be forever. At home our bags were already packed, and my mother shared the news that we were leaving to go to Louisiana with her. We were excited to finally get to go out of town with our mother because every time she went to work, we would stay home with our father, but this time we are going with our mother.

A trip that we thought would be only a few weeks, eventually turned into a few months, then into a few years. To be away from our home in California for such a long period of time wasn't normal for us. This was confusing for any 9 year old because our parents were divorced and we didn't even know about it. While we were away with our mother we spent the entire summer break with our father, things between our parents seemed to remain normal. Maybe in my own subconscious I wanted to think that someday we would all go back to California and life would be as I knew it before we left out of town. I suppressed the fact that things would never be normal again, and held onto the thought that our parents were still married.

After sometime had past, my mother started to date a man. A man that I wasn't too fond of because of course he wasn't my father. Like many other children who are in between two households, I became upset with her. How could she be involved with someone other than my father? I didn't understand it and at the time I wasn't attempting to try to understand. So I began giving this new man the evil eye, ignoring him when he spoke, and just being very reluctant of accepting him into our family.

After all I wanted our family to work, for our parents to be together in the same home, I found myself defending my father's place. Not knowing what all was taking place, this divorce impacted me greatly, I no longer felt whole anymore. After seeing this new man around more often, it began to create a void in my life, and I ignored the possibility of ever seeing our parents together again as a family unit.

In a little over a year, my mother, brother and I packed our luggage once more to move to Georgia. It was so beautiful in our neighborhood, the sight of huge cherry blossom trees and the fresh smell of the rain in the spring. The festivals in downtown Atlanta during the summer, watching the leaves change colors in our backyard during the fall, and to see snow for the first time in the winter, gave me a sense of hope to adjust to a new environment. Familiar with living in the California dessert, to see four seasons was new and exciting for my brother and I.

CHAPTER TWO

Don't Believe The Hype…

The excitement quickly faded once I entered my new school. The students were so cruel, and were picking on me every chance they could get. To be one of the tallest girls in school didn't help either. Students would call me Ronald McDonald, because I had a longer shoe size than the average girl. Some would even call me chocolate chip because I had really server acne and it didn't feel good at all. I was known as the black girl who talks white. Such hateful words were coming from students who looked just like me. Two legs, arms, eyes, and ears but yet treated me as if I was so different from them. This transition became more and more difficult for me to adjust to this move. It didn't stop in middle school, the bullying had gotten even worse once I entered high school.

I didn't have the latest fashion but our way of living was comfortable. My mother worked long hours to provide the similar living environment that we had in California. Regardless of our parent's economics status, the students always found something to taunt me with.

In spite of how much someone tells you that words don't hurt, the truth is that they do. Hateful words tend to leave deeper cuts and though as hard as we try to heal these mental wounds, somehow these words find their way back to the forefront of our minds. It is the power behind cruel words from your peers, and the painful feelings behind it that sticks with you.

The students at school continued to reject me and not include me in the in-crowd. It began to make me feel empty inside. So I buried my head in my school studies, I remember one of my mother's friends telling me "It's a sin to be pretty and dumb" and that stood out to me throughout my later teenage years in high school. I didn't want to be a beautiful young girl that couldn't read a full paragraph, so I began to engage in sports. What I was doing was an attempt to fill the void. I felt as though I was missing out on something.

As I got older, the relationship between my mother and I was pretty difficult for a teenager and a mother. My mother is a godly woman, who went to church, read her bible, and stood on the word (The Bible). That's great and I now understand that as an adult the importance of standing on the word but as a seventeen year old I was less interested in the Bible and more interested in boys.

I didn't care about the word like my mother did, but it seemed as though she would try to beat it in my head. I was more worried about the new Luke CD that was coming out, keeping up with the trend, getting the latest gear, and the hottest shoes. I wanted to be more popular, less bullied, and try to enjoy my teenage years. But trying to enjoy life didn't work because what I wanted didn't happen the way I wanted to. Though my parents played an active part in my life, I still felt as though I had no one to comfort me through this emotional pain that I continuously felt.

May 25, 2002. "Yes!" I screamed to my four best friends during lunch time at school. We were all excited about the anticipated day that finally came. Our graduation day! Sitting around the lunch table we began sharing with one another the activities our parents had planned for us after graduation. About the dresses we were going to wear, what time to meet up for the after party, and who needed a ride. The school bell rang letting students know that we had five minutes to head to sixth period class. Every senior graduate that I passed by was talking about the graduation parties in the hallway while I headed to my last class.

During sixth period block, I pushed my completed assignment to the edge of my desk and began to watch the clock. It seemed like the school dismissal bell wouldn't ring fast enough, I couldn't wait to go home and ask my mother the ultimate question that every teenage girl has in the back of their minds. I was so nervous to even bring up the subject to my mother. Many times I've attempted to have open conversations with her, I longed for her to be my friend.

When I knew she would fuss at me, I would slide letters under her door instead of face to face encounters. Stomping to my room with the letter in her hand she said, "Desiree, what is this? At that moment, I began to question myself if I should've written the letter to her or not, "a letter mom," then I continued to say, "I just want for us to be able to talk as friends sometimes. I didn't write the letter for you to be upset with me." "Mom, you said that we could talk about anything, but every time that I've tried, the conversation ends with you fussing at me." Her response wasn't the one that I expected, "Desiree, I am your mother, I am not your friend." In the same breath, looking me right in the eye, she said, "We are not on the same level, we don't hang out, you're my child and I am the parent." She placed my letter on my desk and walked out of my room. I held back my tears that soon started to roll down my face. I slowly got up from my bed, grabbed the letter and put it in the shoe box where I kept all of the other letters that I've written to my mother. Without hesitation, I started to build a wall, broken piece by broken piece, to block the thought of ever having a relationship with my mother.

On my way home from school, anxiety started to build up, faster and faster. A four minute drive that now seemed to be a long ten minute drive, I was replaying over and over about what I was going to say, how I was going to ask my mother. My hands started to sweat, I told myself "You can do it." To have a boyfriend was the first thing on her list that she was against me having.

I took a deep breath, built up enough courage, and went for it. "Mom", I said with a low tone. I've taken another deep breath and utter the words, "When would I be able to start dating, I am seventeen years old now". "Joseph is nice, tall, he has his own car, and…" In the middle of me describing the boy of interest she said, "You are not in school to date boys you're in school to get an education." "You have your whole life ahead of you to date boys, I would hate to see you waste it all just because you want to date this Joseph guy."

I remember sitting down at the dinner table and listening to the stories of how long my grandmother made her wait until she was allowed to have a boyfriend. I'm sure there are many that may have heard the same things from their parents. It wasn't until my last semester of high school that my mother slacked up a little bit and granted me permission to date Joseph. I was extremely happy because on my graduation day my mother would finally meet the boy that I was so in love with.

Joseph and I didn't attend the same school. Often times you would find students from neighboring schools attending other school functions. When Joseph came to attend my basketball games, I would have this butterfly feeling in my stomach. I was so attracted to his thuggish demeanor, the way he would walk into the gym with all of his friends, his bad boy style, pockets full of cash, shiny bling around his neck, flashy car with 24 inch rims and the loud rumble of the bass in the trunk of his car.

To be introduce as Joseph's new girlfriend and to be finally noticed as the coolest girl amongst my peers at school was highlighted more than my academic and athletic accomplishments. Before I dated Joseph I was known as the girl who had a 3.8 GPA, great basketball athlete with no social creditability. A nerdy church girl, whose parents held her up in a box, the big foot girl who no one wanted to date. What teenager wanted to graduate high school with such a lame reputation like that? Not me!

There was an emptiness inside of me that I naturally felt obligated to fill with something whether it was negative or positive, it was going to get filled. If I didn't fill this void with positive ingredients like education, a relationship with God, purpose, vision, family, I'd slowly fill it with the streets, drugs, robbing, and stealing. All of these things were automatically drawn to me because I lacked the wholeness that I've longed for.

The divorce left a void in my life. I began to fill that void with anything I could. I was feeling so empty even though my family loved me unconditionally and the environment I live in didn't display emptiness.

Luckily it didn't detour me enough to the point of not graduating from high school. I went to my senior prom, when I walked across the stage I felt like I could conquer the world. When I turned to look at my mother when I received my diploma, the look on her face said to me, "Yes baby girl, you did it and I am so proud of you."

Desiree'
2002

CHAPTER THREE

The 11th Time…

      Immediately after my graduation celebration, my mother approached me with a task that I believed to be impossible to fill. She said, "Desiree, now that you are about to go to college and become an adult, I expect you to take responsibility like an adult and help around the house. "I have decided that you are going to pay rent each month until you enter college fall semester." Confused at her request I responded, "Mom with all of the summer jobs taken, how in the world am I supposed to meet such demands in a short amount of time? I want to have fun this summer, plus I only have a few months before the big move to college." As my mother was walking out of the living room she said, "If you can't find a job, then create one.

      I don't know how you're going to pay rent, it is your responsibility to figure it out. But what I do know is, if you don't help out with the bills around this house, I will kick you out. I refuse to take care of any adults in this house."

Feeling a great deal of pressure, I called my boyfriend Joseph. He was one person that I could talk to when my mother and I had major disagreements. I explained to him about the one sided conversation my mother and I recently had with the urgency to acquire such funds before I was kicked out on the street. I was unsure what direction to take because I've never encountered this type of dilemma before. His reaction to the situation was one that no girl next door could ever prepare for.

"Don't worry baby, I have an opportunity for you. Since you have the car, I know a few people in my area and we can hit a few licks (robberies). You'll have the money for the entire summer in no time." He said in such a comforting voice. This method sounded too good to be true, but Joseph reassured me that he and the crew will do all of the dirty work, all I had to do was drive the car. If we were to get caught, I wouldn't get any time in prison, and my hands would be clean. From the robberies I frequently saw in the movies and court episodes on television, I believed every word he said to be true.

I was faced with the decision to go along with Joseph's method of getting money as planned, or anticipate being kicked out of my mother's house. After all, I was down for my man and from the sound of things it seemed as though he was down for me at a time when I needed someone the most.

During this point in my life, I met and ran into the wrong crowd. Joseph quickly began to introduce me to an unconventional way to earn fast money, a new way of thinking. Very similar to the street life that was depicted on television. Everything that my mother had told me, I began to negate. At this moment all of her sayings no longer mattered to me. The way my parents raised me, all of that went out of the window as I started to befriend all of these individuals that I knew were the exact crowd that my parents were talking about when they said, association brings on assimilation. I knew they were bad company but they were instantly filling this void, which made me feel like I belonged to something that was bigger than myself.

Thinking about the colleges I would be attending in a few months, I was very optimistic about my future and my future looked great. I had this crazy idea that if I could fit in with the crowd, have the best outfits, and the coolest boyfriend, I would be remembered as the coolest girl that everyone wanted to be around.

Well, that idea didn't work out as planned. I ended up spending 4 years in prison for this idea and to be honest I didn't like not one minute of it. Instead I was sidetracked by my peers that weren't on track. Two weeks after feeling the greatest highs that I have ever felt, I was looking at the greatest lows that I have ever felt.

On a late Thursday night, I said to my friends, "I'll meet up with you all later, I am about to see Joseph." Tommy, one of the guys that was on our robbing spree team, looked in my direction and said "After the whole team stood up for you against that lame dude every time he put his fists up against your soft cheeks and now you're about to go see Joseph!" He said shaking his head in disappointment. "To think I was so close to putting a bullet in his head after he beat you so badly." I hopped in my car with embarrassment and guilt. "It will only be a quick minute though." I just wanted to hear Joseph's apology face to face. After all he was the one who introduced me to the crew, plus I missed him. It was enough to justify the thoughts that I had of shame to go see him just one last time.

In front of Joseph's mother's house, he entered my car and I said, "Hey baby, did my mom call looking for me again?" His response was a surprise to me, as if he too was concerned. "Yeah, you know that you need to stop hanging out with the crew, these streets aren't safe for you." I mumbled under my breath, "but it's safer with you?" I rolled my eyes and said, "Let's just chill and roll up a blunt or something." Hoping my comment would change the subject.

I knew my mother was looking for me, she had been blowing up my phone and leaving messages for me to come back home. She even had family members calling me. But one message that she left had me worried. "Desiree, this has gone on long enough, I've reported the car stolen, come home now." This was the first time that I have ever been away from home, especially now at this time. I had been away for 2 weeks. Truth is I didn't want to go home, the thrill of the ride was beginning to excite me. I felt as though I was in the movies that I've watched before, and the songs I've heard on the radio. I felt like nothing could stop me; I would be alright because I believed that we were getting to the money. The money that we did have was being smoked up from my new marijuana habit and I still remained on the mission to get enough money in order to pay my mother rent for the remainder of the summer.

Still sitting in my car, Joseph and I were passing the blunt back and forth. He came close and proceeded to kiss me, as if striking me with his fist never happened. Before I knew it I kissed him back and said to him in a calm soothing voice, "Let's go hangout at the pool hall before things get to out of control." I knew if Tommy had gotten word that I forgave him so quickly that things would have gotten out of hand. "All right cool, we can pick up where we left off at later." Confident that our relationship which had been destroyed was once again back to normal, I replied without hesitation, "I love you Joseph."

Soon we were at Bubba's Pool Hall in twenty minute or less. Between the both of us we had already smoked four blunts, I was so nervous for some reason. Maybe because of the fear of my mother finding out what I have been involved in, or running into the crew while we were there. As we walked in, we headed straight towards the bar to get a pair of pool table sticks and the bartender asked for my identification. I was apprehensive about it but I knew Joseph didn't have a driver's license, so I handed my ID to the bartender. "Table 8", the bartender said with shaky eyes. "What is wrong with him?" Joseph asked me. I shrugged my shoulders and said, "I don't know baby, I guess he wanted to make sure my ID was legit or something."

While we headed towards Table 8 to shoot a few rounds of pool, it seemed as though all eyes were on us. As if everyone literally stopped in the midst of what they were doing to look at us. I had a very uneasy feeling in my stomach but I blamed my paranoia on the marijuana that we just inhaled not long ago. I ignored the fact that the robberies we had committed may have been shown on television.

While we were in the midst of playing the first game I looked towards Joseph to say, "Baby, everyone won't stop starring at us, I don't want to stay here any longer." With frustration he replied, "Let's go!" I returned the sticks to the bartender, Joseph right behind me and walked out as fast as I could.

Sitting in the car at Bubba's Pool Hall parking lot with our seat belts on, "What's wrong with you Desiree?" Joseph asked. I turned my head to look out of the rear window as I backed out of the parking space. "I'm not sure, I just had a weird feeling," I mumbled as we were leaving the parking lot. Before I went on the highway, I pulled over to a Texaco gas station to get more cigars. All of the lights were on but it seemed as if no one was standing at the register working. Joseph wanted to go to a gas station closer to his house but I had insisted that he get out of the car and check to see if it was open for service. Joseph got out of the car like he wanted to slap me. He pulled the door at the gas station entrance and yelled back to me, "See, I told you it was closed."

Usually one door is locked because of the time of evening; it was 11:30 p.m. at night. "Go check the other side" I yelled back at him. I didn't feel like stopping anywhere else that night. He walked to the other side and came running back to the car. In a panic he said, "Drive, drive, the police are on the other side of the gas station!" Like a scene from the movie Set It Off, I said, "Damn, calm down. That is how fools get caught. He is just making his normal rounds, that police officer isn't thinking about us." I was so scared because I knew that the police officer wasn't making his normal rounds, he was following us.

We left the Texaco gas station and entered the highway, and the police officer wasn't far behind. Keeping the speed limit as we passed the exit ahead, I noticed two police cars stopped near the ramp. Coming upon the next exit, I saw two more police cars by the ramp. Every exit after had police cars in position, and before I knew it there was a helicopter above us. We were so intoxicated from the marijuana we smoke earlier in the evening, I didn't want to believe that they were in pursuit of us. "Man, we are about to get locked up! What are you doing?! Drive!" Joseph yelled at me because I was keeping the speed limit of 55 MPH. I replied, "Who are they after? They can't be after us, I am driving the speed limit." I wasn't trying to accept the reality that the police were after us, though I knew deep down that they were. If I just drive into another jurisdiction, they will not be able to stop us, right? Suddenly, loud sirens went off, no longer was I seeing the darkness of the night. Instead, I was in the front row of flashing blue and red lights from the police cars that were now surrounding us.

An officer sped up in front of me and abruptly stopped in the middle of the highway causing me to come to a complete stop. Guns pulled out, aimed and pointed at my car. With my foot on the brake and hands in the air, I was too afraid to reach down and put the car in park.

Cops yelling from every side, "Get out of the car! Get out of the car now!" I had an eerie feeling in the pit of my stomach.

In a matter of minutes, all of my opportunities went away. Basketball scholarships that I worked so hard for, disappointing my parents, and not being able to attend my brother's graduation went flashing before my eyes. "I'm pregnant!" I cried back, hoping they wouldn't throw me on the ground. I thought we would never get caught, we got away many times before, and there was no way they would have found us. All of those robberies that we committed finally came to a head and busted in my face.

In the back seat of a police car, an officer asked, "Do you know what you are being arrested for?" as he was checking my identification on the computer in the front seat. "Yes." I answered, leaning forward to relieve the pressure around my hands from the handcuffs. Curious if I was going to confess he replied, "What are you being arrested for?" My response was a surprise to the officer, "My mother reported the car stolen. I mean the car was given to me as a graduation gift from high school and she reported the car stolen in hopes of me returning home." The officer mumbled,

"What a way to repay your mother who worked so hard to reward you for completing high school, and to think that this is how teens these days repay their parents. No the car isn't stolen."

On the way to the police precinct, a flood of tears hit me like a ton of bricks, my mother wasn't trying to get me locked up for a stolen car, she wasn't trying to keep me from having fun with my friends, and enjoying my teenage years. All she wanted was for her baby girl to come home.

Instead of entering college to become an international interpreter or maybe even the next female basketball star. This time I wished I would've listened to my mother, she told me plenty of times that Joseph wasn't a good guy to be involving myself with.

Shortly after eighteen long hours of interrogations, I was escorted by two detectives to the county jail to be processed as an inmate. A convicted felon sitting between four cold prison cell walls. This wasn't on my list of things to become in my future.

July 2002; marked two weeks after I had graduated from high school. As the driver of the getaway car, I was arrested for eleven counts of armed robbery and five counts of aggravated assault. Tommy and Dwayne were the only two in the crew that were always standing up for me during the vicious beatings I received from Joseph. So I felt as though I owed the favor to accept the charges and not say a word.

"Show me who your friends are and I will show you who you will become."

MOM

CHAPTER FOUR

Down The Drain...

Coming down off a high, I woke up in cell 501E to the sound of a correctional officer yelling, "Chow Time!" All you heard was the trampling of feet like a pack of wild horses, all in a race to be first in line. My bunkmate standing over me, said in a deep raspy voice, "Aren't cha going to eat? If you're not in line before the guard passes out the last tray, you won't eat until night." I wasn't sure why no one had gotten me out of this place yet. Ignoring her comments, I rolled over to face the cold brick wall and I started to cry.

In the next few days, I received a visit from my mother. Officer Shelby yelled on the intercom, "Inmate Lee, visitor!" Not sure who was there to visit, buzzed the door of the dorm and directed me towards the visitation area. I looked up towards the visitation area and to my surprise it was my mother waiting on me. As I walked up the short flight of stairs, I started to have this nervous feeling. Entering the visitation area, I sat down to pick up the phone, and I heard her voice. The first words that my mother said to me were, "Desiree, I love you." An overwhelming of tears filled my eyes, with my head hanging low, I couldn't even mustard up enough energy to look up. The words I love you, were words I hadn't heard from my mother in a long time. All of the guilt, and shame weighed heavy on my shoulders. I couldn't bear to see the disappointment on her face. I responded, "Mommy, I'm sorry." As she slowly put her hand on the glass that was between the two of us, I raised my hand to meet hers. This was the first time that I've ever seen my mother cry, as if we both failed each other. I don't know of any parent that would wish ill will upon their child, especially to see them in an orange jail jump suit. It was in this moment that I realized how much my mother and I needed each other. The officer yelled only 2 feet away from where I was sitting, "Inmate your time is up!" We wiped our tears and said good bye.

In my cell I was staring at the concrete ceiling above my bed with thoughts of a possibility of spending 135 years in prison. Would I ever hug my mother again? See my brother's graduation? Ever see my father again? Get married, have children, see the world? These questions wouldn't go away, my thoughts started to taunt me, I felt like I was going insane, like I was fighting in a battle field in my mind. I shouted in a loud angry voice, "LEAVE ME ALONE!" They wouldn't stop, it just kept going and going, one thought after another. I have to get out of here, I said to myself, I started to breathe heavily. My heart just filled with regret, "Why did I get in that car?" "Why didn't I just go home?" I curled up in a ball and cried. My bunkmate stood over my bed to say, "That is one thing we inmates have in common. We all thought we would never get caught." It is unfortunate that I had to find out first hand.

August 12, 2002. On this day I had been in jail exactly 90 days. I was so anxious and my fingers crossed to hear some very good news from my lawyer. News, that maybe I will get to go home soon, but instead I received a letter during mail call. When I opened it, excitement filled my entire face. It read… Inmate 1142980 is set to appear in court on October 2002. I rushed to my cell, got on my knees and prayed. "Father in heaven, please have mercy on me when I appear in court." When I opened my eyes, the cell doors locked and the officer yelled, "Lights out!"

The following day went on like a normal day in jail. The officer would brought toilet tissue and sanitary items to each dorm after morning chow. Every morning, it was the responsibility of two inmates to distribute the items and clean up the dorm, which was determined by cell numbers for that day. Our cell number was listed for today. My bunkmate and I had to take on this duty. I grabbed the bag of materials and began placing them by each cell door. Before I slightly open a cell door, I would peep in to see if the inmates were up. If they were still asleep I wouldn't dare disturb them. I finished the first row and I made my way up to the second row of cells. I went by the first one, and then the next one and the next one. I bent down to reach into the bag to grab the toilet paper and as I lifted my head to peep inside I screamed, "AHHH!" Everything in my hand fell to the floor and the officer quickly rushed into the dorm. She got on her radio and requested back up for medical assistance. Everyone was in shock from what they saw. Another inmate committed suicide. Officers from everywhere were yelling, "LOCKDOWN!" Ushering us back into our cells. The doors quickly locked behind us.

I was so surprised to how fast the officers responded because medical attention to any inmate is very difficult to come by. I remember sitting in the dorm watching the show

The Price Is Right on the television, and hearing screams from the dorm next to the one I was in. It sounded like a whole army was beating on the plexiglass window. We all jumped out of our seats and ran to the main door to see what all the fuss was about. There was a girl who suffered from severe seizures and while all of this chaos was going, the officer was sitting in the booth eating a sub sandwich. Once the inmates in our dorm took notice of what was going on, we began to beat on the window. It seemed like the more we hit the window, the less she cared. The officer turned her chair towards us, licked her fingers, pressed the intercom button and yelled, "It is my lunch break!" Of course her response didn't sit well with anyone of us, everyone proceed to intentionally create a massive riot. In every dorm you saw inmates tearing and destroying everything! Mattresses torn, shredded papers, girls peeing on the floor, flooded toilets, water everywhere! A common method to force the officer to call for help just so the girl who suffered from seizures could speedily receive the medical attention that she needed. We didn't care about the consequences that would follow because her life depended on it. Once those jail doors are closed behind you, no longer are you treated as equal. Our amendment right was forfeited the moment we all made that thoughtless decision that landed us in this hell hole. Now we are treated like animals with a number, like flies around the watermelon at a bar-b-que cookout, dispensable commodities.

Dispensable cattle is exactly what I felt like on *October 2002.* I couldn't sleep at all the night before. I was anxious and nervous as I awaited to appear in court for sentencing in the morning. I was so nervous and scared that I kept my bunkmate awake from throwing up all night. "Here they come!" my bunkmate shouted from the lower floor. Officers entered the dorm, dragging the shackles on the ground, they pointed and said, "Inmate Lee, go to your cell." I walked into the cell, without direction I kneeled down on my knees, and heard the clinging sound of handcuffs. Tight around my wrist and ankles they escorted me to the court house holding cell like a dog on a leash.

A holding cell is where they place the inmates to keep us away from the general public, until it is time to appear in court. I carried a pocket bible in my hands between the handcuffs around my wrist. While I was awaiting my fate, I silently said a prayer, thumbing through the pages of the bible.

Anticipating what the outcome would be like, I thumbed through the pages of my bible and I stopped at the book of Proverbs.

The king's heart is in the hand of the LORD, as the rivers of water: he turned it whithersoever he will.

Proverbs 21:1 KJV

The holding cell door click opened, "This way inmate Lee." An officer grabbed the handcuffs and placed me up against the wall behind a few male inmates. Walking in a straight line with our heads held low we entered the court room. The sheriff then placed me behind the defense table next to my lawyer. I slightly turned my head to see who all came to support me on this day that would alter my life forever. I was overwhelmed by what I saw, the room was filled with my family, members from church, youth leaders, and the pastor of my church were in attendance.

"All rise!" The Judge entered the courtroom. With no emotion the Judge said, "Have a seat." She began stating why everyone was present and told the District Attorney to proceed. With his file in hand, he read off the charges that I was being sentenced for: 11 counts of armed robbery, and 5 counts of aggravated assault. Reality hit me like a bag of red bricks when he described the victims that my co-defendants and I put in danger. I wasn't aware of all of the lives that were affected by the decisions I made, and I was only thinking about was myself. "Judge, Ms. Lee is prepared to plead guilty to all charges and has agreed to accept the sentence of 10 years to serve 7 years in prison." Said the District Attorney.

Who would have thought a young teenage girl from Georgia, with a 3.8 GPA and 2 basketball scholarships, church going parents, could even be involved in such high profile crimes like these. What was she thinking? That's the thing, I wasn't thinking. I wasn't thinking about my opportunities that would have led to greater possibilities. The damage from these crimes cost more than a full ride to college. I was willing to trade my freedom, for a moment of acceptance from my peers. Was being cool or having the validation of street credit really worth it?

At that point it didn't matter how beautiful and intelligent I was, how many friends I had, how much creditability in the streets I had, who my parents were, what church I went to, or what grades and scholarships I received. I had literally given my life, my freedom of choice, over to the court system and now they were in control of what my future would look like.

Helpless, the Judge now controlled the fate of my life. If the state ordered me to sit behind the prison walls for 135 years, the only option I had was to sit behind the prison walls for 135 years. It is unfortunate that I had to go to jail in order to personally see the power of a choice. Imagine if you made a decision that cost you 135 years in prison. How would you feel? How would you feel if I had taken 135 years from your life and there was nothing that you can do about it? It is easy to place blame on someone other than ourselves or to say they made me do it; or to place the blame on our childhood hardships or on the parenting of our parents. I willingly made the decision to drive the car during the crimes committed. Accepting responsibility for my own actions was the hardest pill to swallow. Now it was time for me to pay up.

The Judge looked down at the papers in front of her and started writing. She looked up and said, "Ms. Lee please stand, it is unfortunate that a young girl like you, with so much on the line, committed such crimes. If you didn't drive your co-defendants to the establishments, you wouldn't have found yourself in such a terrifying situation."

Tears rolled down my face. She continued to say, "I am not at liberty to grant you the first offenders act under law. You were fully aware of what you all were doing the first time, the second time, the eleventh time." The Judge lifted her head and looked me straight in the eyes to say her remaining remarks, "I do not know what it is about you; I know once you leave prison I will not see you back in this courtroom again. However, instead of serving 10 years to serve 7 years in prison, I am sentencing you to 10 years to serve 4 years in prison for these crimes committed. If you ever become sad, write me." In that moment, I experienced God's love, mercy, and favor. With my own two eyes I saw how the scripture Proverbs 21:1 was actively applied during my sentencing. Though I was on the road to spend four years of my life in prison, I thanked God that I wouldn't spend 135 years of my life in prison. I was overwhelmed by the Judge's response, the District Attorney met me at the lower podium to swear in my guilty plea and sign my name under the prison sentence rendered.

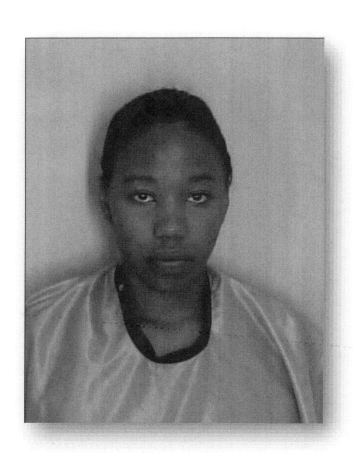

CHAPTER FIVE

3 Quickest Ways to...

Going to prison reinforced every lesson that my parents taught me. The change was when I saw my family coming to visit me, writing me and financially supporting me from the day I was charged until the day I was released. The same friends that I was so loyal to, the ride or die type of friends, were nowhere to be found during my entire prison sentence. Not one came to visit, put money on my books, or write me while I was doing my time. It was my father, mother and brother who loved and encouraged me unconditionally in spite of my short comings.

Like my parents, my brother would often share parables with powerful lessons within them. It was what he said to me during one particular visitation out of many that stuck with me the most. Sitting across from one another he asked, "How are you doing?" "I am alright, I can't wait to get out of this place. Life seems like it is going on without me and that can be frustrating at times." I said with a sarcastic grin. I have to be honest, his response was one that I didn't expect. He leaned forward and said, "When you really think about it, life is not hard at all to understand. Many just refuse to become alive while living." "What do you mean?" I said with a puzzled look on my face. "Well, look at it like this, when a baby elephant is brought into the circus the trainers wrap a heavy chain around the elephant's hind leg and nail the chain about three feet into the ground. The baby elephant is constantly fighting, fighting to free himself from the heavy chain that has him tied down. Because the baby elephant is so young, it doesn't have the power nor strength to pull itself from the chained nailed into the ground. Some time passes by, the baby elephant grows but the bigger it gets the less he fights. Eventually, the elephant stops fighting at all. It becomes accustom and comfortable with being tied down. In fact the elephant now thinks that it is normal because it has been tied down since childhood. Now it has grown to be around 2,000 pounds, and yet this elephant remains chained down by a nail that is only three feet deep into the ground. All the elephant would have to do is pull a little harder and it will be free from the chain and bondage, but it doesn't pull." My brother takes a sip of his water and continues to say, "This elephant would much rather remain in this captive circumstance with the excuse of, that is all it knows. This scenario is parallel to life today, many have already given up because they have tried before and failed. The difference now is that many have now grown but yet use the excuse that it is too hard, or this is how it will always be. Desiree, like the elephants chain, do not allow the prison walls to frustrate you. You have grown, you are not 17 years old anymore. Pull the chain a little harder." My brother's words of wisdom got me through most of the toughest days during my sentence.

When I was in prison I saw the most horrific things. I remember running out of my cell to screams of a young girl getting raped with a plunger in the utility closet. In prison, I saw a person get killed because she refused to be another inmate's "do girl." A "do girl" is a girl who does any and everything for another inmate. There were riots over a stick of gum, and I also saw an inmate burn a young girl in the face with an iron. There were times that I saw inmates sit on the yard to wait until you received your commissary from the prison store, just to take everything from you. Anyone would be lucky if they made it back to their dorm with a bag of chips left. You have to remember that I was in a place for 7 days a week, 24 hours a day, with women who had life sentences and nothing to lose. I was with woman who had families that forgot about them, and they were angry that someone out in the civilian world still remembered that you were in prison.

There are many who have mistaken prison for a place that only those who committed violent crimes go. Assuming that the quickest ways to go to prison are if you murder, rob, or sell drugs. It is true that you will go to prison if you are involved in any of the crimes listed above, however those crimes are not the quickest ways.

The three quickest ways to go to prison is to be dishonest, disrespectful, and to lack respect for authority. Someone who is dishonest will lie, steal, and cheat. A disrespectful person has very little concern towards what you do or who it would affect around you. If a person is dishonest and disrespectful the result will always be a lack of respect for authority. If a person does any of the three things listed above (dishonest, disrespectful, lack of respect for authority) they would quickly find themselves in the same familiar place that I once was in for 4 long years.

How do I know you may ask? Not onl from my own personal account, but there was young girl who found herself serving a two year prison sentence for being dishonest and disrespectful about stealing and using her mother's credit card to rent a car to hang out with her friends out of town. If she was only honest with her mother, I am sure that her mother wouldn't have filed charges of identity theft. If she would have respected her mother and asked permission instead of sneaking, I am sure that her mother would have allowed her to enjoy a trip out with her friends. The decisions we make are so important because they will quickly alter your path towards the future destination, and once they are made, there are no start over buttons.

It's not as easy as a multiple choice test, where the answer is listed amongst alternative answers below. There are only twelve months in one year, twelve months to be 10 years old, twelve months to be 15 or any age. The truth of decision making is that you can't go back and start over. Knowing what I know now, how I wish I could go back and start over. The way life is set up, I can't be 5 years old anymore, and I only had twelve months to enjoy it. You only get one chance, so take advantage of it!

Warning does comes before destruction, and I just might be someone's last warning before making a destructive decision. I spent my time in prison planning how I would take advantage of my second chance once I was released from serving my time. It was in that moment that I vowed to never go back to prison because I could not bear taking my parents through another traumatic situation like that again.

Night and day I wrote in my journal about going back to college to obtain a bachelor's degree, working at a company, saving money, buying a house, and starting a family of my own. When I walked out of the prison doors on my release date, I ran face first into a tall brick wall. My plan crumbled when I encountered the list of limitations I now had because of a criminal background.

CHAPTER SIX

The Lady with the Mustard Seed...

I immediately felt the repercussions of the 11 counts of armed robbery and 5 counts of aggravated assault convictions. A criminal record will never go away regardless of how much time a person has served in prison. The limitations are many; a convicted felon can't attend school because financial aid does not approve a person with a background checks. There are over 46 careers that require a person to pass a background check and exam in order to obtain a state issued license. During the apartment application process, the question is asked if the renter has a criminal background. The requirements for remaining on parole or probation and not returning to prison for the remainder of your sentence are: a person would have to maintain employment, live at a residence, pay restitution, and report to a parole or probation officer monthly.

How does one overcome and become successful beyond the boundaries of a criminal background when the threat of returning to prison haunts them daily? If you don't have a job, you will go to jail. If you don't have a place to live, you will go to jail. If you don't have the money to pay restitution, you will go back to jail. If you don't have a car or bus fare to report to a probation officer, you will go to jail. Though one may only spend 18 months, 3 years, or even 10 years in prison, the fact is we are convicted felons for life. The possibility of an inmate returning to prison is within three years from the date released.

With a determination not to return to prison, I kept searching. During a long six year time frame, in need of employment, I went out every morning, location after location, to only hear, "Sorry ma'am, but we can't hire you due to your criminal background." Disappointed, I tried again the next morning and the next morning, so much that I began to go into interviews expecting the interviewer to respond in the same manner as the previous establishments.

I decided to try my luck and apply for a waitress position at a seafood restaurant. After hearing the word "No" time and time again, I decided to avoid the question, "Have you been convicted of a felony in the past 7 years?" on the application. The manager over looked that section during my onsite interview and hired me for the position. She looked up with a smile on her face and said, "You start on Monday." With tremendous gratitude I responded, "Thank you!" She proceeded to inform me of items that I would need to begin training, white shirt, black pants, non-slip shoes, and a license to serve alcoholic drinks to the customers. "Our restaurant is subject to inspections from the county, to be sure that our waitress' are in appliance with the set state regulations." She continued to say, "You will have 7 days to go to the county courthouse to obtain your license." I replied, "Thank you again for this opportunity." I left excited about the chance to finally gain employment.

The same day I went to the county courthouse and filled out the paper work to obtain an alcoholic license to serve. I came across the same question that I avoided many times before, "Have you been convicted of a felony in the past 7 years?" Hesitant, I checked the box yes and in the lines below, I explained what happened when I was 17 years old. I handed the completed forms to the clerk and waited for a response if the forms were accepted or not. "Ms. Lee," the clerk called me back to the front. "Due to your criminal background your application has been denied, however you have a chance to appeal it with the board. We have a date for tomorrow morning if you are available." Going through this time and time again, I wasn't surprised. "Sure, I am available tomorrow morning." Maybe, just maybe, this time the board members' decision would be different from the responses I've received many times before.

I arrived at the county courthouse 15 minutes before the scheduled time. With sweaty hands, I entered the conference room, the 6 board members were present. Standing at the podium, one of the members spoke, "Ms. Lee, we understand that you are here to obtain an alcohol license to serve." I said, "Yes sir, I am." I took a deep breath and began to explain my situation. "Recently, I have been hired as a waitress after an extensive 5 year job search. I am here today to ask the court to grant me permission to obtain an alcohol license to serve in hopes of regaining employment." Their response was unbearable. One of the board members said, "Due to your criminal background, we are unable to grant you permission to obtain such license at this time." I replied with tears in my eyes, "Okay, are there any alternative options for a convicted felon who is in search for employment? I've tried multiple avenues, and have run into a brick wall."

Another member of the board answered my question in a sarcastic tone, "Well sweetie, what about a hair stylist?" "I've attempted to apply for financial aid and was denied the opportunity to attend college due to my criminal background." I continued to say, "Also, I am unable to receive the state issued license to style hair. Thank you for your time and consideration." Silence filled the room as I proceeded to leave the court room.

I sat in my car and cried uncontrollably. In this moment I felt defeated, lost, confused and hopeless. Nothing was working, I thought to myself, "My life is over. Will anyone give me a chance to get my life back on track?" I went from a day of excitement to a low of disaster. While I was driving home, I made up my mind to give up. I was so tired of fighting. I was tired of fighting against the dream of regaining my life back as a person and not a convicted felon.

I was tired of just being tired. It seemed as if the option was non-existent. Just to think that if I had made a totally different decision when I was 17 years old, not to be the driver of the car. If I would have just gone home and faced my responsibilities, my life would have painted a different picture than what I was seeing in that moment. A different decision would have rendered a different response. Why didn't I just listen, now I have this criminal background for the rest of my life, and I was suffering with no hope left to keep going on with my life?

It had been a long time since I last prayed. So filled with anger, hurt, disappointment, I was unsure of what to say. "Lord, I am tired. Where are you? I need you now, I don't know what to do. I've tried everything and nothing seems to work. Door after door is closing right in my face. What is it that you want for me to do? I am lost." These were the words that I mustered up the courage to say behind the tears that wouldn't stop flowing. I sat there in the middle of the floor and waited. I waited for a sound, for a voice, for a sign. Nothing.

Minutes later my mother called me down stairs and asked me, "Hey, do you want to go with me to the nail salon for a pedicure?" No one knew how depressed I was, nor of the hardships that I was dealing with internally. No one even knew of my thought out plan to commit suicide. Thinking that this may be my last moments with my mother I said, "Yeah, I'll go with you."

Inside the nail salon, I waited next to a lady who was reading a book. She had such an amazing glow with a very peaceful presence. She turned with a smile and said, "Hello, how are you?" I wasn't in the mood to talk, to respond was the least I could do. "I'm okay," I said in an unbelievable tone. She started to tell me about how she walks every morning to pray, and that today she decided to read a book to take her mind off of the daily work load. I blurted out, "Well, I'm a convicted felon and I can't seem to find a job. I am so stressed out." I'm not sure what made me open up to her and say that. She smiled, grabbed my hand and said, "Let's have coffee tomorrow at the café around the corner." I agreed. My plan was to end my life, but it was God's plan to begin to live my life.

At the café, the lady was sitting at a small table in the corner. I was so glad that she invited me to coffee because I really needed someone to talk to, strangers to one another, I didn't think I would see her again after this talk so I let it all out. "I've been going through a lot these past years and encountered many disappointments. It seems like the harder I try to stay on the right path, the more I get knocked right off. No one is willing to give me a chance and I am so tired of going through this pain after I already did the time for my crime." She took a sip of her tea as I continued. "I don't know what else to do, I tried to go to school and I was denied. I tried to get an apartment and I was denied. I tried time and time again to get a job and I was denied. I even tried to get a job and McDonalds and guess what, I was denied." She took another sip of her tea, as if she wasn't surprised by what I was telling her. Not participating in my pity party she said, "It seems to me that your problems are stacking up into these huge mountains." "Yes!" I said, finally someone who understands. "Oh, I completely understand honey." She said reaching down in her purse and she pulled out this tiny jar filled with yellow seeds. "Do you know what these are?" "Of course, I do" I said sarcastically. "Those are mustard seeds," remembering the sermons that I heard in church as a young girl. "I know already, with a mustard seed of faith you can move mountains." I didn't come here for someone to preach to me. To my surprise she didn't preach at all, she said, "Honey, this is all the faith you need." "And to be honest, this is all the faith I have left." I said with a little attitude, because she didn't give me the response that I was expecting after I've just poured out all of my problems to her.

She said, "Here, open your hand and put these mustard seeds in your purse. So that every time you reach in your purse it will remind you of how much faith you need." Desperate for some answers on how to overcome all of the obstacles that I was facing, I took the mustard seeds and put them in my purse. "Now every morning I would like for you to begin your day in prayer, read these positive affirmations aloud, and I will follow up with you in a few weeks to see how you are doing." I must admit, I was doubtful of any changes coming from this but I said to myself why not? I will give it one more chance before I call it quits for good.

He replied, "Because you have so little
faith. Truly I tell you, if you have faith as
small as a mustard seed, you can say to this
mountain, 'Move from here to there,' and it
will move. Nothing will be impossible for
you."

Matthew 17:20 NIV

When I woke up the next morning, after prayer I pulled out my notebook with my affirmations written down. I said out loud, "Today is a great day! I walk in peace, with confidence and authority. Everyone who I come into contact with will see God's love through me. Everything that I do today is done in love. I own my own power to create and be well in mind, body, and spirit. In all of my thoughts and attitude, I have the power to create my own peace. I can do all things through Christ who strengthens me and supplies all of my needs. I am whole and healed, forgiven inside and out. I have faith and I walk in faith."

"Today I am thanking and uplifting myself for all that I have endured, in my growth and development for my greater good. I have no obstacles and I command my mountains to move."

No longer was I having days of disappointment and doubt, instead it was more days of love and peace. Thirty days later, I received a call. I usually don't answer calls from private numbers, but something told me to answer the phone. "Hello?" I said in a low tone. The caller replied, "Hi, can I speak with Desiree Lee?" "This is she," confused as to what this call was about. "Yes I am an officer from

DeKalb County and I wanted to know if you would be willing to share your story with some students at the local high school." I quickly responded and said, "Yes." After he gave me the details of the event, I immediately called the lady with the mustard seed.

"Oh my! You will not believe this! For the past thirty days, I've done exactly what you asked me to do. Pray in the morning, say my affirmations, and water my mustard seed with faith. Well, God is using my pain and directed me towards my purpose. I've received an opportunity to share my story with the students at a local high school." Over excited about my breakthrough, I couldn't get it all out. I reached in my purse and a mustard seed was caught in my nail, at that moment I remembered all the faith I had left. She said, "Wow! God will do exceedingly, above, all you can ever ask or think!"

"Desiree, I want you to know that when I was going through my mess and I couldn't see any way out, a lady gave me a mustard seed and believing just that much, I was able to overcome a huge pile of adversity." My mouth was wide open. I replied with tremendous gratitude, "Thank you so much for not giving up while you were going through your darkest moments, because my life was depending on your faith."

There are times when we are going through some of the most trying times in our lives that it will seem as if the world is caving in on us. As if we are the only people who may be going through the roughest hardships, to the point when we want everyone to join with us in our pity party. But I want to inform you that even in the midst of that dark cloud, you can't give up because there is someone who is depending on your faith. What if this lady would have thrown in the towel? The result would have been my life taken, because my life was literally depending on her faith to preserver through her storm.

DESIREE LEE
MOTIVATIONAL SPEAKER

CHAPTER SEVEN

The Brightest Light in the Darkest Place...

Believing just one more time was the only option I had. How can God make a way out of no way, if you haven't been in a no way situation? Very often we ask God to make a way and soon after we've prayed, we get in the way in an effort to try to 'make it happen' ourselves. I've been guilty of trying to 'make it happen' on many occasions. Does God (all knowing, all powerful) need our help? He is God all by Himself. Sometimes it is best that we just be still, let go, and let God.

Once I applied my affirmations daily, the perception of this disaster began to change. My way of thinking soon transformed and I saw clearly the resources that were right in front of me the entire time. When I was still, I started to see the possibilities in the impossible. I became enlightened over the very things that were stifling my success. Wow, I thought to myself in amazement!

My friends, I know that it may seem impossible, as if you can never catch a break with tragedy. Day after day drama, bills, and problems keep coming your way; everything stacking up so high that they become your mountains. How do I know? Because it wasn't long ago that I too found myself in that dark place. Speak to your mountains and they will move! *For words are vibrations. Vibrations are energy. Energy is power.* Therefore the words that you speak carry more power than we really give credit to.

It is the light, the power in our words that will brighten the darkest places. Giving up is no longer an option for you my friend. Regardless of how awful the situation is that you're in right now or how young or old you may be, there is always an opportunity to turn that situation completely around. With a ten minute decision, we have the power to alter any outcome of a situation when we decide to make an alternative choice. When we decide to believe just one more time, miraculous things happen.

What changes when a person has made up their mind to make a decision that will alter the negative outcome of their situation to a positive outcome? Here is what happens, when they finished having a pity party, they got up, they knew it had been done and because they knew it had been done, there was a new belief about this barrier that was once unreachable.

Nowhere around you may look anything like success. When you shift how you look at the situation around you, it is your faith that interprets the surroundings and alters your perception of what was once an unfavorable situation. The glass that was once half empty is now half full. You might say, "Desiree, it's not possible. I'm finished, I can't do it, and I've surrendered. I've faced rejection again and again, I've tried over and over again. There is no such thing as success, success is only for a small class of people. I am throwing in the towel."

Yes, things do happen in life that you could never anticipate and many times when those things happen you want you give up. Trials will offer you justifiable reasons to give up. But giving up is not an option, just like the lady with the mustard seed, there is someone out there in the world who is depending on your faith to preserver through the most difficult obstacles. There is someone in the world who is depending on you not to give up making the vaccine for cancer. There is someone who is depending on you not to give up to create a prosthetic limb. There is someone who is depending on your faith, not to give up on starting that small business that will employ millions.

What if Martin Luther King Jr. had given up during his fight for equality? What if George Washington Carver was so tired, that he chose to give up while producing more than 300 products from the peanut? What if Oprah Winfrey allowed fear to hinder her from going the audition for 'The Color Purple?' What if President Obama doubted that he would ever become the President? What if Steve Jobs never fought his way through depression after his own friends took the very thing that he had work so diligently for? What if Henry Ford gave up when his neighbors taunted him as he engineered his truck in the garage? What if they all, and so many more, decided to give up while facing some of life's most difficult barriers? But they didn't, they all preserved because in one form or another we were all depending on their faith.

Guess what Ladies and Gentlemen, that's what we have to do with our dreams, our goals, our visions; you cannot give up. The tiny seed knew that in order to grow, it needed to be dropped in dirt, covered in darkness, and struggle to reach the light. You have to go through, in order to see the light. There is some child, some teenager, some parent, and some family out there who needs for you to shake off the pain, to shake off the fear, shake off the doubt and get back into the fight.

My friend, pick up that towel and use it to wipe the sweat off of your face. In spite of how I felt from facing rejection after rejection. In spite of how horrible things may have looked. In spite of what others may have said, I found a place within myself where nothing is impossible. With my mustard seed in my hand, I kept going, thinking, knowing, and believing that it was possible. I continued to see by faith, not where I am now, but where I one day will be.

I've decided that I could no longer sit back in that dark place and allow myself to be comfortable or complacent with poverty, pity and mental imprisonment. Defeat is merely a state of mind. The first thing that I had to do was imagine the possibilities. I was so tired of going through disappointment after disappointment that I made up my mind to imagine so INTENSELY that the imaginations created a new reality, instead of hardships with a criminal background. These affirmations that I had "spoken" daily (*Words are vibrations. Vibrations are energy. Energy is power*) affirmed my imagination to overcome the limitations with a criminal background. I got up believing and knowing in my heart that it is possible.

We as humans have something that no other animal has, and it is called imagination. Your imagination allows you to see it before it actually is. I need you to see yourself becoming the person that you want to be. You have to live as if it already is, block the whole world out, put some music on, some classical music on, go to a library, and block the whole world out. The problem that some of you may have is that you are living in the past and you're living in the present. You continue to talk about the mistakes, talking about your past, talking about your trials and I want you to know that everybody who has ever been great, has had an obstacle that they had to overcome, a barrier that they had to climb. There is no individual that has ever reached success who didn't have to go through an obstacle. I need you to go into your future every single day, and imagine what you're going to become.

Imagine what you are going to be who you are becoming. So you have to use your imagination and your imagination has to take you beyond the pain, your imagination has to take you beyond the trouble, your imagination has to take you to the next level. We have to see ourselves there, long before it happens.

Muhammad Ali once said, "I knew that I was great, before I was."

You must embrace faith, I had to believe that the things that I see years from now, 5 years from now, one day that very idea, passion, dream is going to be successful. When I was bullied in school, I could have quit. There were many days that I thought about committing suicide, but I said to myself, "Desiree just keep imagining, keep creating, keep believing, keep seeing what you're going to become."

You know what I've discovered, when you're working towards your dream, your goal, sometimes there will be no one around to encourage you to keep going, nowhere around you do you see anything that looks like success. When there is no evidence around you, when you have pain in your life, when you are tired and feel like giving up, you have to clinch tight around your faith and believe just one more time.

Like David in the book of Psalms, you have to encourage yourself, you have to believe that although it is not happening right now that if you keep pressing, if you keep pushing that one day the doors are going open for you and what you imagine will become your reality. But your dreams will never manifest if you give up. If you quit now you will never have the opportunity to see your dreams become your reality.

While you are on your journey towards a successful future, if it may be on your way to college, promotion on your job, starting a new business, even getting married, understand that there will be some people that are so unhappy with themselves, that they will say, mock, and do heartless things to remove your focus and get you off track. Whatever you do after you encounter these meaningless comments, do not belittle your gifts to satisfy their unconscious insecurities. Never allow those who are not on track get you sidetracked from Gods original plan for your destiny. Do not allow distractions to distract you from stepping into your greater.

There is a scene in the movie "Life After," starring Will Smith. In this scene, Will Smith's character said something that stuck with me. He said, "You must realize that fear is not real, it is a product of thoughts that you create. Do not misunderstand me, danger is very real, but fear is a choice." When you embrace faith, fear automatically becomes a non-existence. The fear of failure, "This might not work" attitude or the fear of succeeding, what if it works? I might not be able to handle it. Faith is what eliminates fear.

Have you ever wondered why God references a tiny mustard seed to faith? What some may not know is that a very tiny mustard seed grows into a tree that is about 20 feet high. It has a root system that overtakes everything in its way. If there are weeds, trees or any other plants, the root system will engulf that very thing until it's no more. This particular root system is very much parallel to faith. Once you've decided to cultivate your faith, walk in faith, talk in faith, to believe just one more time, immediately you will see how your faith has overtaken the doubt that was once there, overtaken the worry that was once there, overtaken every obstacle that was once unreachable. Cultivate and nurture your faith so well that those fears will no longer stifle you from reaping the 20 foot harvest that you've been longing for.

Decide to see with your inner sight and not your outer sight. When you make up in your mind to no longer allow those very things to hold you back, when you get so tired of going through your situation over and over again, the decision to stand will push you into the greatness that you had all along. You will no longer see things from your outer sight but now see things from your inner sight. No longer will you see the glass as half empty but half full. No longer will you see things upside down but right side up. Why? Because you see every situation that you may face from here and until forever more through the eyes of faith and not from the vision of fear.

I want you to get into a place in your life where every mistake you've made, every set back you've encountered, every obstacle that you haven't overcome, every barrier that you've not climbed, and embrace it. If you've failed a class, lost a job, started a business and it doesn't work, don't stop, don't quit, get back up and try again. Hold on to your dream, hold on so tight onto the imagination of what you want to become until you become it.

CHAPTER EIGHT

Imagine, Create, Become...

The goal isn't to live forever, the goal is to create something that will. We are all creators! Would you agree that God is in everything and everyone? It is difficult to describe the ultimate universal power of the all-knowing God. God is all powerful (omnipotent) and all knowing (omniscient). He is also able to be present at all places at all times (omnipresent). God is the ultimate Being in existence, creator, perfect in power, love, and character.

To know this, we can agree that God lives in the trees, the air, in every plant, He lives in you and in myself. To have a just merely a piece of God's existence within us, then we too are Great, we too are powerful, we too are creators. When God spoke and said, "Let there be light," it was so. Therefore whatever we speak it is so. For our words are vibrations, vibrations are energy, energy is power. So speak to your mountains and they will MOVE! Speak to your problems and they will MOVE! Speak to your fear and it will MOVE! Speak to your doubt and it will MOVE! For there is power in your words and when we recognize this authority that lives within us, the authority to create and destroy, the authority to speak life or death, the authority to speak that very dream into existence, then and only then will you overcome and rise above the very thing that is stifling you from stepping into your greater, from stepping into your purpose that God has placed inside of you.

Take a moment to look around you, everything was created from within. From a piece of paper from the trees, the shoe string on a shoe, a straw, even this very book that you are reading. What is stopping you from creating something great that will live forever? Someone said, "I want to create," this or that and it was so. If we were to explain to Abraham in the bible about the functions of a computer or the functions of a cell phone, I am sure his response would be unconventional. I know his response was parallel to the responses that Steve Jobs, Oprah Winfrey, Judge Greg Mathis, Jennifer Hudson and many more received. They mustard up the courage to create beyond the circumstances that surrounded them. With that same courage they didn't allow the mountains consume them but saw from the eyes of faith that one day the entire world would see what they believed in from the beginning. To see what they created from their imaginings of becoming great. They forgot about all the reasons why it wouldn't work and believed the one reason why it would. Courage is being scared to death, but saddling up anyway. Open your eyes to the resources that are available around you and do the best that you can with what you have until you can do better. Shift your focus on the one reason why it will work and you will be amazed of the results and what you are really capable of. You are capable of going far and beyond because God lives inside of you.

I remember flipping through the channels on television and I came across a show called Super Soul Sunday on the OWN Network. A phenomenal speaker, Dr. Wayne Dyer was speaking on the subject of the power behind two words. These two words are the most powerful; for what you put after them shapes your reality into what you become.

The words, "I Am." I Am Great. I Am Brilliant. I Am a family person. I Am a hard worker. I Am a man of my word. I am brave. I am whole. I am dependable. These very two words are true in a negative context also. I am sad. I am scared. I am unworthy. I am a failure. Be very mindful of how you use your "I Am's," for it is the name of God.

There is a parable in the bible about Moses and the burning bush. Moses was tending to his flock of sheep in the dessert and came across this burning bush that wasn't consumed by the fire. From this burning bush God had spoken to Moses and told him that God heard the cries of His people that were enslaved by Pharaoh (the king of Egypt). He then told Moses to go to Egypt and tell Pharaoh to free the Hebrew slaves. In the book of Exodus (NIV), chapter 3:13 - 15 reads:

13. Moses said to God, "Suppose I go to the Israelites and say to them, 'The God of your fathers has sent me to you,' and they ask me, 'What is his name?' Then what shall I tell them?"

14. God said to Moses, "I am who I am. [c] This is what you are to say to the Israelites: 'I am has sent me to you.'"

15. God also said to Moses, "Say to the Israelites, 'The Lord, [d] the God of your fathers—the God of Abraham, the God of Isaac and the God of Jacob—has sent me to you.'

"This is my name forever, the name you shall call me, from generation to generation."

Dr. Wayne Dyer encourages us to change the way how we habitually use the two words I Am when he wrote this, "Run through as large an inventory as you can of the things that you would like to define your life. Then make the shift in your imagination from an I am not or I am hoping to become, to I am. You want what follows I am to be congruent with your highest self, which is God. Beginning with your inner dialogue, simply change the words that define your concept of yourself. Redefine your self-concept by choosing the words that you opt to place into your imagination. Try this rewording of your inner world as a beginning step to accessing the assistance of your higher self and fulfilling your desires."

Here are some suggested avenues that helped me in transforming my negative outcome from the criminal decision I made at 17 years old, into a positive outcome that changed my way of thinking and inspires others.

Dr. Wayne Dyer suggests that, "Instead of I am incapable of getting a job, shift to I am capable. Similarly, replace proclamations of I am not able to live in peace with I am peace. I am unlucky in love is replaced by I am love. I am unworthy of happiness becomes I am happiness. The words I am, which you consistently use to define who you are and what you are capable of, are holy expressions for the name of God—the highest aspect of yourself. Break lifelong habits of unwittingly besmirching this holy name. Discontinue using pejorative labels to cast aspersions on your holy self. Always make your very first consideration the honoring of your Divine spirit. This will allow you to rise to previously unimagined heights. Teach your outer self to accept the unlimited power of your inner spirit and the things you place in your imagination can become true for you."

Imagine who you want to be, use what you have to create what you want to become and speak it into existence. What does this mean? From the molecules, cells and atoms that make up your body, even your mind will tell your body to line up and transform with the words that you speak. The enemy is not concerned with your current position, it's your potential that scares them. Your potential, drive, ambition, is the very thing that P.U.S.H. (Pray

Until Something Happens) against that brick wall to overcome life's most difficult barriers. There was a time that I couldn't go over this wall because I was a convicted felon. I couldn't go to the left nor the right of the wall because of my criminal background. They said I couldn't go under this wall because of my criminal background. So guess what, I saw the wood laying off in a distance and built a ladder to climb over that very wall that everyone said was impossible for me climb.

Who told you that you had to wait to become a millionaire, to become successful? There are many young people that have reached a level of success while they were teenagers.

"The only limitations one has are the ones they place on themselves"

Muhammad Ali

What is difference between young people that are successful and the young people who are not? Successful people narrow their focus solely upon the dreams and goals that they wish to accomplish. No longer do they choose to hang out with the crowd that doesn't implement success, nor do they continue to partake with those who emulate destructive behavior such as doing drugs, shoplifting, sneaking out the house, staying up late at night, or being disrespectful to their parents or authority. To take the same funds and the same time to invest in a successful future in effort to create something so dynamic other than waste your time and money on things that don't add value to your future goals.

You too can become a dynamic innovator. You have a computer, cell phone, hands, legs, and a mind. You have the same tools that some of the greatest innovators that ever existed had when they started. It is time that you stop playing around with life because time is not waiting, nor is time playing around with you. So it is up to you to take advantage of what you have. Right now you are in the best position to become successful. It's never too late to become what you could have been.

One of the most common things that I've encountered with young people and adults when

I travel nationwide to deliver my presentations at school assemblies, youth organizations, conferences, and various other platforms is that everyone can agree on is this, "I wish I would of listened to my parents," "I wish I would of taken advantage of the opportunities that were placed before me." "I wish, I wish, I wish." Trust me you do not want to regret saying the same thing. Take advantage of what you have now, believe in where you will someday be, and actively take the steps towards your dream destination. A year from now you will wish you would've started today. What is stopping you? Stop saying I wish and start saying I will.

It has been said, "The harder the battle, the sweater the victory." Victory is good. Why? Because of what you've become in the process is far greater than your dream. The kind of person you've become, the character that you've built, the courage that you've developed, the faith that you've manifested, the people you have inspired because you didn't give in when the battle got tougher.

I could have allowed my criminal background to demolish me, to tear me up and spit me out. Instead I took that very thing, the criminal background to prevent others from going through what I have been through and inspire those to overcome the barriers that have resulted from past decision making. I chose the service of love.

I truly believe that I went through this experience so that no other person would have to, and to provide a chance for parents to rebuild relationships with their children, and create a blueprint for those who are searching for direction on how to eliminate the very thing that is holding them back. When I lost all of my excuses then I found my results. You may have encountered many defeats but you must not become defeated.

With this book, I present to you a gift of love, faith, and peace. The world is bigger than what you see in front of you. So ladies and gentlemen, from here on out, begin to dream above life's most difficult barriers! You're too close to give up now. You have come too far from where you started. Be courageous and take the limitations off.

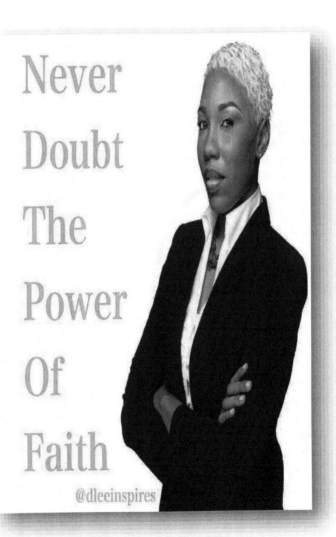

CLOSING REMARKS

Equipment

Figure it out yourself, my lad,

You've all that the greatest of men have had;

Two arms, two hands, two legs, two eyes,

And a brain to use if you would be wise

With this equipment they all began.

So start from the top and say "I CAN."

Look them over, the wise and the great,

They take their food from a common plate,

And similar laces they tie their shoes,

The world considers them brave and smart,

But you've all they had when they made their
start.

You can triumph and come to skill,

You can be great if you only will.

You're well equipped for what fight you
choose; you have arms and legs and a brain to
use, and the man who has risen great deeds to
do. Began his/her life with no more than you.

YOU are the handicap you must face,

You are the one who must choose your place.

You must say where you want to go,

How much you will study the truth to know;

God has equipped you for life, but He

Let's you decide what you want to be.

Courage must come from the soul within

The man must furnish the will to win.

So figure it out for yourself, my lad/lass,

You were born with all that the great have had,

With your equipment they all began,

Get hold of yourself and say: "I CAN."

~George Washington Carver

REFERENCES

Proverbs 21:1 KJV

Matthew 17:20 NIV

Muhammad Ali Quotes

Exodus 3:13-15 NIV

Super Soul Sunday- OWN Network
(Dr. Wayne Dyer Episode)

Equipment – George Washington Carver

"I wouldn't want any teen to go through what I've experienced in prison! I wouldn't want any parent to experience what my parents went through seeing their child in prison!"

Desiree Lee

ABOUT THE AUTHOR

A Phenomenal Inspirational Story

Public Speaker| Author| Philanthropist

Desiree Lee is a renowned keynote speaker, author, and philanthropist. Using herself as a visual aid, Desiree has committed her life to provide a prison prevention workshop, with resourceful tools others can apply to their lives, in effort to overcome life's most difficult lessons. It is designed to derail young people from making decisions of crime and transforming our youth into rewarding citizens of society.

Delivering a high energy message which helps the audience retain the image of heading down a criminal path, with a message of inspiration wrapped in a package unlike any we've seen before. Not the typical "Scared Straight" approach, instead to show people how to eliminate fear, seize opportunity, and live up to their greatness.

Desiree is one of the nation's leading authorities in connecting and stimulating human potential, utilizing a powerful delivery and newly emerging insights to awaken, inspire and channel people to new heights of achievement.

Desiree's personal mission in life is to inspire to individuals who feel that they can't overcome their current barriers. Ms. Lee travels nationwide presenting her presentations, "Imagine, Create, Become," Ms. Lee also teaches the steps to "Eliminate Fear and Become Fearless" along with presenting the "Season of Preparation: Seize Opportunity & Step into Your Greatness" workshop!